P9-BZQ-763

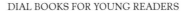

DIAL BOOKS FOR YOUNG READERS
Published by the Penguin Group
Penguin Group (USA) LLC
375 Hudson Street
New York, New York 10014

USA / Canada / UK / Ireland / Australia / New Zealand / India / South Africa / China

penguin.com

A Penguin Random House Company

Text copyright © 2014 TransKids Purple Rainbow Foundation
Pictures copyright © 2014 Penguin Group (USA) LLC

Library of Congress Cataloging-in-Publication Data

Herthel, Jessica.
I am Jazz / by Jessica Herthel & Jazz Jennings ; pictures by Shelagh McNicholas.   pages cm
Includes bibliographical references and index.
ISBN 978-0-8037-4107-2 (hardcover : alk. paper)
1. Jennings, Jazz. 2. Transgender people—Biography. 3. Transgender people—Identity. 4. Transgenderism. I. Jennings,
Jazz. II. McNicholas, Shelagh, illustrator. III. Title.
HQ77.7.H467 2014   306.76'8092—dc23   [B]   2013031939

Manufactured in China on acid-free paper
1 3 5 7 9 10 8 6 4 2

Designed by Mina Chung · Text set in Cooper Oldstyle

The publisher does not have any control over and does not assume any responsibility
for author or third-party websites or their content.

This artwork was created using watercolor paints.

I Am Jazz

by Jessica Herthel
&
Jazz Jennings

pictures by
Shelagh McNicholas

DIAL BOOKS FOR YOUNG READERS an imprint of Penguin Group (USA) LLC

I am Jazz!

For as long as I can remember, my favorite color has been pink.
(My second-favorite color is silver and my third-favorite color is green.)

Here are some of my other favorite things: dancing, singing, back flips, drawing, soccer, swimming, makeup, and pretending I'm a pop star.

Most of all, I love mermaids. Sometimes I even wear a mermaid tail in the pool!

My best friends are Samantha and Casey. We always have fun together. We like high heels and princess gowns, or cartwheels and trampolines.

But I'm not exactly like Samantha and Casey.

I have a girl brain but a boy body.
This is called transgender.

I was born this way!

When I was very little, and my mom would say, "You're such a good boy," I would say, "No, Mama. Good GIRL!"

At first my family was confused. They'd always thought
of me as a boy.

As I got a little older, I hardly ever played with trucks or tools or superheroes. Only princesses and mermaid costumes.

My brothers told me this was girl stuff. I kept right on playing.

My sister says I was always talking to her about my girl thoughts, and my girl dreams, and how one day I would be a beauuuutiful lady.

She would giggle and say, "You're a funny kid."

Sometimes my parents let me wear my sister's dresses around the house. But whenever we went out, I had to put on my boy clothes again. This made me mad!

Still, I never gave up trying to convince them.
Pretending I was a boy felt like telling a lie.

Then one amazing day, everything changed. Mom and Dad took me to meet a new doctor who asked me lots and lots of questions. Afterward, the doctor spoke to my parents and I heard the word "transgender" for the very first time.

That night at bedtime, my parents both hugged me and said, "We understand now. Be who you are. We love you no matter what."

This made me smile and smile and smile.

Mom and Dad told me I could start wearing girl clothes to school, and growing my hair long. They even let me change my name to Jazz.

Being JAZZ felt much more like being ME!

Mom said that being Jazz would make me different from the other kids at school, but that being different is okay. What's important, she said, is that I'm happy with who I am.

Being Jazz caused some other
people to be confused too, like
the teachers at school.

At the beginning of the year they wanted me to use the boys'
bathroom, and play on the boys' team in gym class, but that
didn't feel normal to me at ALL.

I was so happy when the teachers changed their minds. I can't imagine not playing on the same team as Casey and Samantha.

Even today, there are kids who tease me, or call me by a boy name, or ignore me altogether. This makes me feel crummy.

Then I remember that the kids who get to know me usually want to be my friend. They say I'm one of the nicest girls at school.

I don't mind being different. Different is special! I think what matters most is what a person is like inside.

And inside, I am happy. I am having fun. I am proud!

I am Jazz!

TransKids Purple Rainbow Foundation ("TKPRF") was created in 2007 with a commitment to enhancing the lives of children born with Gender Dysphoria. TKPRF is committed to the premise that Gender Dysphoria is something children can't control, and therefore, society needs to embrace them. Families need to support their children and allow them to grow up free of gender roles. TKPRF is dedicated to helping trans youth by sponsoring gatherings and specialty programs, providing scholarships to transfriendly camps, donating money for research, helping homeless youth, and providing financial assistance to other trans youth organizations. Jazz is an honorary co-founder of TKPRF and actively educates society by appearing in the media and speaking at schools, universities, medical schools, conferences, conventions and symposiums.

Find out more at www.transkidspurplerainbow.org